A Short Supply of Viability

A Short Supply
of Viability

Annette Gagliardi

A Publication of The Poetry Box®

Poems ©2022 Annette Gagliardi
All rights reserved.

Editing & Book Design by Shawn Aveningo Sanders
Cover Design by Shawn Aveningo Sanders
   (photo via Creative Commons License)

No part of this book may be reproduced in any manner whatsoever without permission from the author, except in the case of brief quotations embodied in critical essays, reviews and articles.

ISBN: 978-1-956285-15-4
Library of Congress Control Number: 2022906654
Printed in the United States of America.
Wholesale Distribution via Ingram.

Published by The Poetry Box®, July 2022
Portland, Oregon
ThePoetryBox.com

*In memory of
Anna and Oscar Stabnow
and
David and Gloria Gagliardi,
who taught us new worlds,
through their respective illnesses.*

∼

*To all caregivers whose tender mercies provide a better life
for those drowning in the ever-rising waters of decline.*

Viability

def: ability to work successfully;
the ability to survive or live successfully,
perhaps to flourish—be fruitful, and multiply

When we see the declining physical condition of our loved ones (and then ourselves!) it can be easy to lose sight of viability—especially when it seems to be in short supply-- meaning living successfully may be short-term or that living is not optimum, not easy, not pleasurable. The transition from optimal life to death may be a slow decline or a quick get-away. But, either way, there are adjustments to be made.

Viability is still present in the transition, its shadow casting sidelong glances at us from darkened corners, challenging us to move on with life, taunting us to be happy, if even for just this moment. Can we look at the facts of dying and still go on with our lives? Yet, we must go on until the very last breath—and beyond.

Sometimes the person who is physically declining is in better condition than the caregivers who live with the stress of grief and myriad other incidentals that attach themselves as they go about the days and nights 'taking care of'. They lose the joy of the moment, the measure of the seasons in the challenge of taking care. I ask you: *Who's to say it isn't intended that way?*

As our loved ones approach the next phase of being, we ponder the meaning of life, of death, and what might follow. There is pain in growth and pain in death. It is a fact of life. But that doesn't mean the pain isn't worth it. Go on. Share the pain. Read a poem and weep if you feel the need. Weeping cleanses your *gutters to a slim, polished newness.*

This book provides viewpoints to ponder, glimpses of lives well-lived and not well-lived, but still works in progress. It gives the caregiver's perspective as well as the perspective of those being cared for—both, in various stages of viability.

Contents

The Death that Duty Brings

Celestial Call	15
How Vast the Universe	16
"I am asleep, but my heart keeps vigil"	17
Apotheosis	18
Classic Sinatra	19
Resurrection	20
Distant Thunder	22
Gourmand of Orange	23
Stopwatch	25
Carrying the Pain	26
A Minor Theft:	
A String of Pearls	27
Alzheimer's	28
Mumbled Moments	29
The Value of Forgetting	30
This World is a Grave	31
Geraniums	33
Dreams	35
Grief in the Sail	38
Flamingos	37

Things I Can't Remember

Lacuna	41
Contradictions	42

Rose Quartz Heaven	44
Unknowable	45
Wants or Wishes	46
Mother's Ring	47
Fresh News	48
The Sea Shifts	49
Failing Total Recall	50
Hard as Stone	51
Liminal Spaces	53
Dates	54
My Lover Waits	55
An Illusion	57
Uses for Ashes	58
incubation	59
A Dried Bird's Nest	60
His Floured Past	61

Quicksand

A Siloed Ecosystem:	
Before Dawn	65
Left Unsaid	66
Residue	67
A Short Supply of Viability	68
I Feel Your Pain	69
The Vehicle of My Heart	70
A Convenient Death	71
The Cost of a Limo	72

Pondering an Imponderable	73
She Was the Black Starling	74
A Tenable Demise	76
Benevolence	78
A Trilogy:	
Water Turned to Ice	79
Mirage	80
Whiteout	81
Saline	82
Burgundy Shapes	83
The Daggered Ice	84
January Wolf Moon	85
A Single Sparrow	86
Dissolution	88
Death Is Not Personal	89
Lift Me Up	90

Resources	93
Acknowledgments	95
Praise for *A Short Supply of Viability*	97
About the Author	99
About The Poetry Box	101

The Death that Duty Brings

Celestial Call

White clapboard siding tells the tale
of religion—*this church* seen better days.
The arched stain glass lit from within
doesn't begin to shed illumination

on the surrounding outside, nor does it hide
the dirty bell snugged-up against the
front vestibule like a helmeted soldier.

The northern lights cast ethereal brightness
to the scene, while the stars rotate
their ornate destinations, but fail to mention

why the tower balcony is boarded up—
the bell demoted to its lowly berth.

A steeple, sans cross or weathervane,
lies asleep, windows shuttered and
closed, like the congregation
no longer present to witness, or care.

It seems, no one is home there.
Yet, God still beacons, using celestial light
to bring us back.

How Vast the Universe

    The end is near;
It's raining while I grieve.

It rains while disdain changes to regret
    slides down . . . slides on down.

O little drops, I dismay
    at your constancy,

steady in a way that only begins
    to tell—a whisper in the rain.

It rains while the morose, listless me
    fades to washed-out loneliness.

The roaring thunder shouts the rain
    away from the crowded streets,

meets me, runs down my cheeks, soaks,
    drenches, seeps into pores,

    cleaning my gutters
to a slim, polished newness.

"I am asleep, but my heart keeps vigil"
—*Song of Solomon 5:2*

The soft shelter of slumber
rests upon my breast,

all that's left after
the murder of innocence.

Witness the martyrs
suffer for their faith.

Why should we suffer?

My heart waits. Its pain
framed in a dream.

I watch, ever alert
yet, peacefully passive.

I snooze in the sanctuary -
my anchor, my port.

I dare to doze;
defend my dozing.

I drift off while
the day draws near.

Be merciful, oh Lord.

Apotheosis

The Milky Way's culmination
of light, intoxicating parallels
co-signed, the continuum sequenced,

marks the echo of stars
sung a million years ago
along an etched surface—

sounds of tranquility.
Heavenly hosts signed
and marked this trail

the Milky Way navigates.
Unannounced promises lie
in the lines between passages.

The horizon reveals & hides each next
moment, submerged in depths of regret,
moist, unaware and orgasmic;

our vain attempts
are damp and futile
—a silent good-bye.

Classic Sinatra

Frank died the same day
Mom did, their essence

mingling with the marrow
of others meeting their own demise.

Sinatra might have been singing.
Mom might have been humming along.

The slaughterhouse barely opened—
its barn-red paint flaking in the sunlight,

decay and deterioration running rampant
among the bodies of those left behind.

Rotting wood floors no longer holding
the necessary weight to carry on.

Medications bulldoze and demolish any scant
health left. Bodies razed like aged sheds

in abandoned fields, slow-dance
with dying, no longer trying to pilfer

another long day, butchered and broken
into mingled segments of back story.

I choose to think Mom and Frank sang
and danced the night away in that old barn.

There might have been dragonflies.
The sun might have been shining.

Resurrection

My husband and I own a small plot of land
overlooking the Mississippi, near Highway One-Ten.

Only now it is called the Crosstown Highway Sixty-two.
The land moves like a memory alongside that small, still dose of
    water.

The grass is so short it doesn't move,
so long it bends and leans into the shifting breeze.

It reflects from the hill off the placid water down below.
You could roll down the hill into that pool

or sit down next to the slab with your ancestor's name,
the date, the graphic, the metal flowerpot.

That land blurs ancestry—
creates a smudge of colors that obscure;

creates the calm, the peace, the tranquility
for those resting—residing in repose.

All one can see is the land in green pixelated colorscape—
The territory below the land speaks softly of newer colors.

These acres have got more soul than the blues;
more soul than Willie Nelson's harmonica player—

He's been stuck underground,
serenely playing between gigs, for years now.

Everything here is formed in relationship to every other
living thing around it. Each are everywhere and nowhere—

from East and FAR east to West and Wild west
from DEEPEST North to deeper south—

lying here   resting here,
easing into the land.

Distant Thunder

The morning is impressed with itself.
Sun peeking over the horizon, winks
in another page in the book of this life.

A barely escaped death is as good
as it gets when everyone scratches
the ground for goods.

Life is a short struggle, sometimes shorter
than we wish—hoping things happen for the best—
at least that's what we are led to believe.

Even if we are the earliest bird in the bunch,
time hops ahead of us. Have we only wept
for the days that scorched as they flew by?

What of the time spent fulfilled? The banquets
of spring and summer spent raiding
feeders and flying freely?

Even those days we've kept as roses
in a bouquet are a slow simmer of stew,
served up with a fortune cookie

that provides a lesson in some way,
forecasting our fate whether we
acknowledge it early—   or late.

We might end up like the lowly worm,
circling our wagons underground—listening
for distant thunder.

Gourmand of Orange

He bit into it like someone
eating their last meal,
savoring the lush treat,
licking the dripping rind,
smacking his lips as he
appreciated the tangy aroma.

He sucked the color from the
room as easily as that tangerine—
its ripped rind left
lying on a white napkin—
his attention diverted
from the fruit.

He sucked the orange off
the roses, there on the table,
arranged so elegantly in the silver teapot
with a wide, organza ribbon;
He swilled the fragrance as he went,
nodding a reply to my soft argument.

Yet, he had no awareness
of how he left things;
how the tangerine was left
lacking its color,
the residue dry and smooth
as a coffin lid.

The air was thinned to a wisp
with others left to gasp
for the remainder,
the flowers, devoid of perfume

[. . .]

or hue, washed and wasted—
even the ribbon left defiled and

distant   tarnishing the teapot.

Stopwatch

cutting time
        mechanically
with its little saw

wood fragments
        like toothpicks
knit the day

time's little droplets
        fill flowers
inside out

drizzles of dust
        without oasis
file and fill

tiny night noises
        cut time
slice seconds

mince the minutes
        that fall like leaves
cleaving lives

into cut rate and cutthroat
        yesterday—today
before and *after*

Carrying the Pain

She carries her hatbox
like a purse, its silver

strap slid over one arm,
then the other.

She shifts the weight from arm
to arm as she tires.

Sometimes that silver strap trembles
on her shoulder,

like a waterfall of tears
streaming from a summit.

The grief inside—*her treasure,*
never out of sight, nor far

from her touch.
She fondles her prize;

caressing as she goes.
I can hear her dead birds

weeping softly from inside
her hatbox.

A Minor Theft

A String of Pearls

like bunny beans
dropped on my lawn—each owns
a memory. They call,
remind me—but not her.

The photo of someone she
knew, but does no more—
it's scrolled frame slipping
away in degrees as she
holds it in her hands.

The small trinket rubbed
smooth, while she forgets
the retelling of why it means
what it means to her.

Those hands worry
treasures that signify something
stolen—
one small theft at a time.

What has left her bereft, sitting
in her chair, only aware of the blur?
—not the hour, the day, nor the pearls
that she leaves   as mine.

Alzheimer's

is the snake in the grass
that lasts past midnight
and hides in the sleeve
of your new green dress—
the one you wore
for your high school prom
and took in after you
lost the baby.
Those snake eyes
glitter; its tongue
flickers like the ones
you wore when your father
taught you to dance—
your feet slipping after
his paced steps.
You wept when he died,
his funeral a great pyre
of grieving—widowed women
bemoaned his passing,
as well as your mother.
But here he is again, visiting
you in your hospital bed,
with the rose-red pillow
you adore, wet with tears
of suffering and grief.
Yet, who will look after him
while you stay bedded down?
You must get up and cook
the meal—and kill that
slithering snake.

Mumbled Moments

obstinately tenacious
cling to what's left
of my mind.

Mysterious memories
half-gone in a twinkling,
rise and submerge
while my mind unwinds.

All that I've lived;
my life, or what's left—
its memories gathered
suddenly left behind.

Mention the name
of my lover and spouse
and hope that
I catch it in time.

Touch me just so,
as if you must go.
—I'll whisper
that I will be fine.

The Value of Forgetting

The lure of
knowing
is a lie.

To understand the
value
of forgetting,

one must enjoy
ambiguity
and feel its

bliss.

One must observe
ambivalence
in any measure,

live
with inexact
decisions,

and study
failures' alternatives
freely.

This World Is a Grave

It was Jude Nutter who wrote,
*The world is a grave. With all its exits
barred*.[1] And I wondered
how she knew at such a young age
the vagaries of existence—
the desolation and destruction.

I wondered how she knew the cost
of living a life that seems daily like a death—

our contrite confessions aside, there must be more
that allows us to soar above our mundane
toil than this coiled, curling crypt.

I wondered how anyone ever knew
this and why more of us are not scarred
or scared shitless.

How do we carry on surrounded by this gilded gyre—
its din of clutching beetles and maggots
running rampant in the darkness, spilling
disease and unrest, famine and fear.

This world that takes from, wants from, needs
—siphoning the soul one ounce at a time,
hollowing out until only a shell is left, a single
carapace as reminder of what might have been.

---

1 First lines of "Epitaph on Interstate 80, Nevada" pg. 37 of *The Curator of Silence* by Jude Nutter.

I remember a family gathering
hugging and mugging with cousins and siblings,
reminiscing and celebrating aunties and uncles, yet

amid the laughter feeling so lonely—
            so very alone—
that I had to hold myself tightly
in check to keep from *stepping out* —

I had to stop myself from running
down the highway. I had to focus on
NOT screaming, *this world is a grave!*
And I understood:
There are no exits.

Geraniums

Wilted blooms drip
red on my deck.
I break them off at the stem
without remorse
and wipe their stain clean.

> *Each morning a gentle hand*
> *with moistened towels*
> *wipes the caked blood*
> *off Mom's lips.*

Dry, withered leaves
are plucked
and discarded from my plant
in the same manner.

> *My mother's lungs*
> *are dying on the vine*
> *with no way to pluck off*
> *the dead members.*

I slide the pot East,
turning it to get the full sunlight.
I use the water hose to
drench the plant,
flooding the pot to the brim.

> *What was done today? I ask*
> *the nurse as she slides the comb*
> *through Mom's hair and*
> *straightens her robe.*

[. . .]

Then, I go inside,
to admire the view
from my window.

*Her wheelchair is pushed
to the window
where the morning sun
warms her and soothes.*

Dreams

She was laughing in the photo
her hair blowing in the summer breeze.
Her body akimbo and loose.
She spent those days easy and relaxed

in jumbled play and imagination.
She raced the wind in the meadow
and climbed the mountain that
was the willow tree, then hid

in its branches to discuss the latest
boy who infatuated her.
She lays long in bed these days
loath to give her body the workout

getting up will require.
The oxygen hose attached and
organized helps her breath
well enough to hoist herself

out of bed and make it to the chair.
She sits to dress and pauses
amid the going, contemplating
the girl in the photo—

Grief in the Sail

Sunlight illuminates today,
yet grief shades
my way like the awning
over a window.

I watch your pain, the slow-
quick unwinding
of your life. It cuts deep
furrows in your brightness.

Small glimpses of who you
used to be emerge-recede
like dolphins in the sea.
I watch the boats inch their way

from the harbor and know you
are on a similar vessel moving
away—
always away.

You are meeting the horizon
so very soon. No room for pity—only
grief in your sail
along with the evening tide.

Flamingos

In the last glow of the day, flamingos
       stand on mysterious girders
as though time were a commodity stretched
              beyond the horizon.

Like rose-colored statues
        soaking up the evening sun,
    as it rolls over the water,
            reflecting their crimson spectrum.

And now, one bends and dips
        her S-shaped neck into the waters
           that have been here for eons,
    rich with foraging crustaceans.

No one has tried to paint
      their ruby hues nor count the feathers
on a single vermilion wing,   yet the path
          to heaven is not born in shades of scarlet, nor lined
with plumes of red.

    What will I do, when that special
          bird lifts its ruby wings to fly?
And how can anyone know that she is my dearest
         adversary who has come   to stand
    in my own home waters?

When you shelter your rival
      do your feathers reflect the sun?
         And who will take me in when my feathers
begin to redden?

Things I Can't Remember

Lacuna

There are blank spots in my skill set,
certain threadbare   patches   in my measure.

    I'm no longer able to come and go as I please,
    yet, I must   let it all go in order to maintain myself

    or kick myself   dead in order to live again.
    There are things that need saying so the saying can end.

I host a tiny measure of regret for the boys
I might have said *yes* to

and polish the unintended consequences
of the boys given my *affirmative action*.

    I was the snap of flame lighting the day's candle,
    the ring of morning breaking the still of dawn.

    I was the roller-coaster at Treasure Island,
    riding fast and furious—screaming with high adrenaline.

But now, what's leftover smoke sifts out of the room,
silent as the evening breeze   and as sincere.

Contradictions

Mom got smaller and smaller,
losing weight like we all wanted to,
yet her needs got greater and greater

filling up our time like foam insulation,
sprayed into every crack and crevice.
She could only stand one or two people

in her room at a time, yet more and more
of us were drawn into servitude
to possibly satisfy her every urgency.

She ate less and less, yet we brought
more and more food for her to eat,
which was stacked in her frig, around

her room and by her bed. She tasted
or slightly nudged at it and nibbled,
still losing weight as she 'feasted'.

She needed fewer clothes, yet we
purchased new again and again,
first one size, then another

as her body changed. We bought new
shirts and sweaters with front buttons,
then no buttons, pants with elastic waists,

larger socks for ease of slipping on her tiny feet,
bigger slippers, softer slippers, different
colored slippers, then smaller slippers;

all with the hope of pleasing her,
of making her more comfortable.
Yet, her requirements changed

daily and we were forever needing
to do, to get, to fix one more thing.
Until the end, when all our activity

stopped abruptly and we were forced
to pack up and put away all that busy
we had used to keep her with us one more day.

Rose Quartz Heaven

On a walk near the stream
that meanders through my woods,
I stood and listened to the water
giggle and splash near my feet.

I bent to pick up the small rectangle of rock
that caught my eye. It was heavier than I thought,
a six-sided stone layered, stepped in places
with a clear, white center. Red striations
draped its top and bottom.

I imagined myself alone
inside the stone, *the world at my feet*.
The sun shone through the quartz,
casting its rose-window glow,
its crust of crimson shading me.

I breathed inside the stone for an eon.

Finally, I eased out under the hem of red,
placed the rock back on the forest floor,
dreamt my life again.

Unknowable

      The mist meanders around the bend
of day, leaving a trail no one can follow.

      —So much is uncertain;
such a mystery.

      Where does the doe hide
her fawn?
      When do the disappearing stars
sigh their song?

Is the universe controlled
      inside or out?

Our concepts of mastery
      only a mirage of mirror and light.

The doe grazes in the quiet
      field, drinks from the stream,

allowing access to the unseen,
      not minding being led.

Wants or Wishes

I am the lonely outpost, the last stand in a long line of laments.

Seconds snatched; minutes smuggled
from a fast-framed, film-flickered life
leave no room.

How do we let go of our own wants, while fulfilling those of others?

Years gone with not even a millisecond
left for ransom—
as if you care to be aware.

Does your emergency necessitate my doing something?

Save & store the energy, drive, emotion needed.
Fulfill a single one
of your own wants or wishes.

Will you feel pleasure or pain?

NOWHERE   is the place
between disbelief and disappointment
left with less than a breath.

Who's to say it isn't intended that way?

Do the heartbeats used
for those dreams destroy
lives lived in spite of them?

Would you languish for that loss, as well?

Mother's Ring

The diamonds are small—
barely glints along the silver
band's slim, simple smile
circling my ring finger—not the marrying
finger. The one on my right hand.

Dad was poor—heck we all were.
But he always said, *Only the best
for your mother. Spare no expense!*
knowing that he could
afford nothing, yet somehow
getting her heart's desire every time.

The tiny diamond chips set
into the swaled cleave signify twenty-five
years wedded tether.

It became mine—to remind me
to love through the good and bad.
They were married over forty years before
COPD took them within three
months of each other. If that isn't

love, I don't know
what is.

Fresh News

This morning the dew sparkled on the fresh-grown grass
and the yellow tulip I have been observing, has opened

into full-flower and spun its gold into the universe
as a way of reducing the damage.

A young Cardinal sang its first song, which was returned
in kind, and while I sat contemplating nature's gifts

the Holy Spirit joined me and confirmed that *all
is well and all is well, and all manner of things are well.*

Cancer spins through my blood, meandering
its way around my body unfurling its majesty.

The sun slides over the edge of today, white-lighting its
way upward and flowing in all directions as if

viability were water. Only light and water can flow like
love into hearts and bodies, minds and cells—

except for the big "C" that flows while investigating,
castigating, conquering and devouring

each cell encountered—
its sparkle marking the trail.

The Sea Shifts

Back up.   Look.   Keep looking.
The sun moves slowly and swiftly,
edging toward the horizon.
Keep looking still—squint a little.

It is not the sea that shifts,
yearning to swallow the sun,
growing swollen with want
compounding.

Sunlight, whose folds ensnare
our quick sluice of thoughts,
plunges afire to ground,
sweeps underneath the horizon

like the snap of a trigger
beneath a chemist's torch.
The light flickers and dies
as the whole world ticks

toward the sound of applause.
Giving way to flowering darkness,
shadows flicker across the water,

along with hours lost down the drain
of the day. The smell of summer sun
still sits in our hair,

on our faces and with our
utopian dreams.
A fresh evening breeze
bestows a tiny limit to regret.

If food is what you want,
eat now.

Failing Total Recall

I am the dripping water
swirling round the sink's drain,
circling again and again in rapid,
then slow, carousel spins—

each circle, the journey of a lifetime,
the trip of travelers long past
and all but forgotten. No.
They are readily forgotten, as
you are—and the man in the moon
who flew too soon to stay afloat.
Down the drain for both of us.

Thwarted in the prime of my life,
dripping oil like a leaky engine,
losing leftovers like a thanksgiving
host generous enough to share
the baked goods that took days
to acquire, create and serve up.

I am the moist repast, used up
and empty—dry to the bone
without time to hone my
technique, or to bone-up on
skill levels that buoy.

I am the water, abandoned; lost
with every twitch and twinge
of arthritic fingers and thumbs,
with no way to climb back
into the faucet of readily available
knowledge amidst this hastily
congealing navigation.

Hard As Stone

my father dug into the Earth in the Black Hills
Gold Mine   two stories underground,
his way lit only by the light on his helmet
with pick ax and shovel   he dug—
pressing his muscles into
each striation of the ground

using the bundles of fibrous tissue on his back and legs
that became layered like the colored ribbons on an agate
becoming what he dug, what he hollowed out

the smooth, polished stone in shades of brown
with mahogany, umber, and sienna ribbons
following each other around the outside
and even though we cannot see them,
they run through the center as well.

what he dug became a cavern   that grew
over time—with each stroke
of the ax   as it cleaved the rock

smooth, yet hard.   hard as granite—
hard as the dark   deep, down in the mine
hard as the days and nights he excavated the Earth
digging and cutting the bedrock,
creating ridges and valleys
inside the world of stone

hard as the life
inside our mother planet
under her crusted mantle
with her breathing herself

[. . .]

onto him and sighing
as he tore away her flesh

hard as it is to suffer patiently
while something or someone
digs you hollow

Liminal Spaces

are usually haunted—sitting
near (and nearer) the center
of each gravitational attraction,
spilling liquid, moist and sumptuous
as holiday pudding,

gravitating leisurely,
so slowly that no one notices
that faint movement—
that coming nearer the wake
of each other's orbit,

a closeness opening
translucent portholes,
loosening aromatic windows
to closed places

that life sequestered,
condensed—viability lasts
      just past the point
of seductive fascination—

the aroma dissipating
in the aftermath
      of each passing.

---

*Liminal: occupying a position at, or on both sides of, a boundary or threshold.

Dates

I make Date Cake every year
for my husband's birthday.

Those dates we purchased in Israel,
carried securely on the plane
all the way home to Minnesota.
Such a long journey;
the smell of dates drifting
about us on the plane, in terminals,
during customs check in.

The smell escaping all along the way
as we carried them home to make
Date Cake with fresh dates
instead of the dried ones usually used.

Such plump, moist, aromatic
fruit I never saw before—nor since.
The distinct texture a soft, sticky concoction
unlike anything I'd seen in the American markets:
dark skin with smooth, flaked-off sections
of paper-thin cuticles not quite fig, not
quite confection.

Like the frail skin of an old lady;
tissue paper inside an unwrapped
present, like my husband's hands
as he lay abed—dying, dying to eat
that moist deliciousness one more

time. Dying to see the sun rise
on another birthday.

My Lover Waits

My lover waits in darkness,
knowing he will find me there.

He calls to me from the deepest,
saddest depths of my despair.

He yearns for me at height of celebration.
He climbs the highest reaches of temptation.

My lover is a patient soul.
When I will come, he does not know.

He waits for my demise
with wise and patient eyes.

Time is of no concern to him.
Still, he bids me enter in.

My lover calls for me to do my part.
His sighs are ever present in my heart.

He waits with patient, panting breath
'til I release this body's hold, by death.

With a velvet soft ring in my ear
a voice of reason so sincere;

He asks one tiny act of will—
would my beating heart be still?

My lover meets me at some distant floating boat.
A long-forgotten melody burns nightly in his throat.

[. . .]

His soft embrace dissolves my burdens here.
He promises all my daily sorrows disappear,

If I just welcome his embrace
and taste the lust of death upon my face.

He suggests that this unbearable life
is filled with too much agony and strife.

In the silken night my lover bids me come;
let us contemplate the stars, becoming one.

I am wooed by his thirst for me.
His passion snuggles tenderly.

My constant lover huddles 'round my soul.
The drumbeat of my heart is his goal.

He is endless as the rain;
his siren song a continual refrain.

His hymn is ceaseless as the moon,
an unremitting devil's tune,

'til death has nobly helped us meet
then into his arms I finally retreat.

An Illusion

your act of kindness
      is illusion

like shadows
      reflected

through hot fusion—
sweat and thrust

      heave and motion
all elevation will become
      collusion

      you pace the moon—
and aid the stranded

planets within your delusion—
      so easily demanding

more and more care,
      so, so unaware—

alive still,
      but not really there,

keeping you bound
      and waiting impatiently

yet necessary
      at least, necessary

Uses for Ashes

Used firewood marries fat,
      sound and strength
      mixed begets soap
scours metal clean
         eventually.

Glowing embers cool,
      then warm what's left
      of dimmed days no longer viable,
save radiant smolder and chunks
         of residue.

Mulched into steep, dead-still soil, snicked and snugged
        into place at hydrangea's feet gets blue roots
truer blooms, also redder,
      richer tomatoes picked
         eventually.

Lay my ashes around your head,
      at your feet, across the bed;
scatter them among stray dogs, Sunday
Sparrows, between sidewalk cracks to mingle
      among the elements

already there.
      Just don't lose sight of them.
I may need them again,
         eventually.

Incubation

unspeakable need
hugs froth and spray
that cauldron together

at the last minute,
bully each other
and torment,

rumble in the morning
mist as muted thunder,
past the sense of it all

and before benefit of any
boy's usefulness,
before need of any

girl's productivity,
like a kernel
tightly encased,

ready to detonate
yet,
tranquil as a cone

on a pine tree
waiting for freeze
and heat to open

the husk
of its armor.

A Dried Bird's Nest

Only dried branches left . . . and fluff.
I thought of you, with the first

drop of exploding snow.
Stars gaze from the milky way—

cosmic voyeurism, the cosmos kissing
my reverie through the night sky,

its northern cold a series of moons playing peek-
a-boo, creating enough white light to play at night

when we dared to stay out past bedtime.
Can I be part of the electric dance that is you,

a sluice of your juice, a part of your whole?
Can I tick with the tocking clock of your heart?

One dried branch of memory left—
and fluff. Only snow-filled fluff remains.

I dreamed of you. Thank you
for not waking me.

His Floured Past

She tells me how he looked back then—
She—with her red hair, white skin.

Just a girl in love, but still aware
enough to know her family

would not accept his inky Italian
blood—would see him as too dark.

Chuckling, she tells how she powdered
him with flour before introducing him.

His full, black hair and she so fair—
his tall, muscular build; her so small

and the flour falling off his
handsome features to his shirt front.

They told her, *Look elsewhere.*
He isn't the one. But he was. He always was.

He held that build to the end,
even as the cancer wasted him;

—kept his muscular frame
despite the chemo's slow spin,

his mahogany skin, smoothed,
faded with the ash of illness.

The streetcar rumbled every night
past her corner—and he on it.

[. . .]

Just far enough away to stay out
of sight—in the light of the streetlamp

he kissed her—and she still
remembers her heart

racing when she and he
hugged the darkness.

She strokes his lush, black hair.
Laughing, she tells the story again.

Quicksand

A Siloed Ecosystem

Before Dawn

the forest is dark　　　　and damp
　　with fog rolling in

we may not last the night—
　　time to break　　　camp

get out of　　　sight—
　　the plight of the masses

will get our asses
　　chewed and bloodied

leave our reputations
　　torn and　　sullied

dawn is a long way off,
　　so don't scoff　　at the darkness

heed the need for speed
　　lest we bleed along with the rest

rain threatens – lightning, thunder
　　promise to pull us under

perhaps we'll drown
　　before the dawn

Left Unsaid

time vibrates embers
of mellow, marbled

musk,
where it

gleefully glides
across the miles

between us;

warps the very
atmosphere,

soothed like
rhapsody's

exuberant window.
it kisses the lip

of your essence,
uncoils the spice

that used
to be our life,

and withers.

Residue

this town's tall chamber
stands still and empty,

like a missile system
deployed and spent,

the name on its face
faded to a shadowed film.

the leavings of a life
well-lived slumbers here.

perhaps it will rise up,
reclaiming animation's embers,

slide cinders together
to meld into

a new order, or *phoenix* alive
in some high, pyrotechnic cataclysm.

what remains is only surplus;
the overage of existence;

only the flora and fauna
that span a siloed ecosystem—

the aftermath of what
created and enlivened.

A Short Supply of Viability

I am the trashcan of detritus filling the hours
of life—the taste of tedium. I am your unmade bed.

I am the parked car idling in the winter—running
engine using up gas going nowhere.

I am the chauffer collecting dry cleaning, mail,
medicine, hair stylist, groceries, mending, car repairs.

I am the Hausfrau gathering these essentials
rearranged once at home. They remain only moments,

then dissipate like condensation in the morning sun.
I tidy pieces of possibilities, spending days,

one heartbeat at a time, suffusing seconds of existence
with minutiae, loading my life with trivialities,

caring for those who need, until I am left
wondering if this constant consideration will sustain.

Will changing furniture or food provide the succor needed?
Until I am left wondering why this treadmill continues

to support us—with viability
in such short supply.

I Feel Your Pain

I don't presume to know the
depth nor the breadth of your suffering,

but my own experience has touched
the surface of that deep pool.

I bleed just as you do. My emotions
simmer in the narrow pot of my

pain, sun shining on grief's
pebbles beneath the surface.

Yet, I feel no compulsion to spew
my desolation into the stratosphere.

The lull of listless melancholy
permeates places in my heart

no-one can reach, even with an
extensive knowledge of sorrow.

You don't need to hear the measure
of my pain to gain understanding.

I need only see your face
to taste your hurting.

The gaze in the mirror
is familiar, and comforts.

The Vehicle of My Heart

carries your pain as well as my own;
a purchase long done   and gone.

Our encounter clings
to steadfast long-suffering;
we ride—as it slides away.

We strive, stretch, stronghold
our way forward, expending
the fuel we might have used to survive,

which gets us no closer to nirvana
than our huddling inside
this cocoon of comfort.

Healing comes later
than we want, yet our hearts
do not go untended.

The paraclete is listening;
rejoice in the consolation
of redemption.

A Convenient Death

I want a convenient death—
quick and painless—

one that leaves people wishing
they'd had even one more day

with me, instead of wondering if I will ever
depart. I don't want to last long, lingering nights,

laying listlessly as family or friends
fake funny repartee by way of entertainment

while bemoaning my sorry plight
in the hallway outside my bed.

Nor do I wish to last past the need
of me, beyond the necessary requirement

of my living for someone else.
Of course, what I want and what

I get may be very different, indeed.
So, let me bleed enough to satisfy

those who need to see red, then,
let me be led to the door of death

to depart without further ado.

The Cost of a Limo

My friend was talking with his funeral
representative and found out it will cost two
thousand dollars for them to carry his body from
the church to the graveyard—riding in the limo.

He thinks a buddy could put him in the back
of his '97 Ford pickup and transport him, with
time to spare and at no cost to anyone.

Who wants to take that two-thousand-dollar
ride at the end of a life filled with more
million-dollar days than one can count,

at the end of a life filled, chock-full
of not-enough-money for much of anything
yet quite-enough-money to survive this
varied existence in all its costliness.

Who doesn't yearn to live *high-on-the-hog*,
riding in style in a black Limo? Yet, what the cost?
Do we save those high-minded moments

for death's delivery? Do we waste our wanting,
worn close to our chest all our lives, then enjoy
the ride of our lives, after our lives are over?

Pondering an Imponderable

If you can pretend that you have a life that will go on and on,
then you can plan for next month, next year, and the millennium.
But if you are diagnosed—or if you're not;
what makes you so sure that life will   go on   and on?

If you can believe that love is real, and the truth
is there in front of you, to do with what you will -
then the thrill of life is the truth of that love
and the belief that love will   go on   and on
until, or perhaps beyond, the end of your life,
no matter what ails or befalls you.

Can you believe (or pretend to believe) that your life
has the truth of love and that love will   go on   and on?
Or are you a disbeliever; so sure that the end is near
and you are so very clear about the happenings
around that event, and its eventuality, which is more dear
than one might suppose?

Then, you must live as if your life will go on and on
without remorse for the course you have chosen,
nor the consequences of your measured path,
that may or may not last past the day or the
evening, which may (or may not)   go on and on.

She Was the Black Starling

    Like an oil spill left over
after the hot summer rain.
iridescent in the sunlight,

not yet afterlife, yet still after
the last breath has flown the breast,
    past the point of no return.

The corpse   scorched into concrete,
    sun-bleached and bare,
lay like bones blanched on some back street.

    Flies hummed a vanishing tune.
Crows, baking in the bleachers, sang *auld lang syne,* rubbing
shoulders while waiting   like old men at a ball game.

    There was no glass in her thought. No transparency.
Yet, she could not have been more clear;
    her mouth pressed against the windowpane of death.

No air was to be found there.
    No breath. No life left to live.
Her harsh reality kissed the shore of leaving.

    Shot at dawn, viability gone;
executed amid the morning's mist;
    the crows and their song descending.

Ants amassed in the concrete
    crevasse beneath her,
their funeral demolition long discharged.

I could not see the desecration the ants had done.
    The starling just compressed
to slack sheet of paper   to dark stain on sand   to shadow.

The day, full of clouds, threatened a moist repast.
Thunder rumbled; lightening illuminated the darkness.
    Yet, no rain came to relieve

termination's hammer pounding—the oppressive weighing down,
the incessant gnawing, gnawing, gnawing—
    removing the last extent of her exquisite existence.

A Tenable Demise

The physical decline of this house is an old woman
whose voluptuousness has dwindled and dried up.

The wallpaper sags like soft skin, covers and uncovers
this place I can never revisit. It peels away

the years, exposes secrets kept
hidden—souvenirs from the past.

Rouged grains of dust cover stained
walls in wither and wilt.

Thickset wall boards are gnarled bones
with cracks that let in the scent of morning,

the fragrance of night; cracks that open
the insides to insects

who crawl and chew, like the mince
of wounds long raw,

mingled with time-cluttered tales
and possessions—poverty's rusted toxins

cheated from the shining sun.
Mice have nibbled and inhabited

bedding—opulent undergarments
surrendered to time. Butterflies

turned to moths have finished
the few crumbs of lace left

shriveled and gasping. The sub-floor is
an exposed path scoured by erosion—

thirty years of second-generation dirt, its digression a slow
pond of decay, incensed by the passage of stolen moments,

betrays the lives lived here; waits for the final fall.
A murder of crows fly away to sing their song

of mourning; consider the banging of the screen
door, and call back a cry of *nevermore!*

Benevolence

You, who snap
under the weight of the moon's glow
on your last, long, lover's lament,
too bent to hear words of affection.

You, who lift
your aspirations toward lovers
who know not your needs,
who bleed with their own poverty.

You, who rise
sunshine stiff with finger's shriveled
from too long in the sun, and run
toward daylight like it's vanishing forever,

Wrap your arms
around sorrow's shank. Sink your teeth
into the nectar of the day. Abide in the sweetness
of the sun & let your pain come undone.

Soak in the love the sun provides;
just be *alive* with its shining.

A Trilogy

Water Turned to Ice

We are fluid as the Arctic
at the beginning of creation
    before God created light
to warm even a thought

inhale without freezing
hold your breath
    under water
search for the shore's surface

rush to reach ripples of air
    gulp some there before
blacking out

solid as a hurricane leveling lives
    one single swoop—
the brittle air an iron bell
    knells the dawn of destruction

stopped cold   the roar
    splash and soak rush together
race the sun, the moon across eons
    into the future

before melting into the taunt
    newly old   worn down,
washed out and whipped,

    alone   treading water

Mirage

There is a certain sunlight,
in the Arctic that reflects and reveals
other lands: cities, mountains, seas,
each glistening mystically.

We know them and we do not.
It sends us dreaming and yearning
into the twilight, each image depleting
as the day drinks the night,

lapping up our hunger—no longer
viable; until the diminishing light
pinpricks that bright vanishing
into the landscape of stunned darkness.

Our dreams are chilled and lost—
frozen in polar wind. Then,
Behold!
Starlight illuminates
what sunlight did not.

Whiteout

—the glare of sun's blaze
on glacial soil

creates invisible movement
untenable life

chipped lines and oilish drips
flecked from palatable whites

spread sparsely
to avoid claustrophobia

all's vain and dangerous—
dreams dying a slow demise

bodies buried amid
Siberian hurricanes

time flows like ice
in the hot sun

we come undone
and run

un-involvement
is colorless

participation
unnecessary

unless we wish
to shift

Saline

salt slid from the tear
of a motherless child whose
orange groves hung heavy
with grief oozed from lips
beyond repair—

edged the ears off
the corn and slipped sideways
to smile at the watermelon
patch whose hatchlings
strutted and stalked, pecked
and pawed the ground in search
of minerals that would induce
a full measure of life—to provide
for and savor the nuances
beyond their control

they would hug all children
to themselves like a bee hugs
the flower, gathering honey
and shedding pollen from
free-floating organisms
whose only purpose in life
is to provide the salt
for grief-stricken tears.

Burgundy Shapes

      slant the doorframe

tri-dentate leaves
    of silver and bronze—triplets

ease along the sidewalk
    of our mortality

heading in the direction
    of deeds and misdeeds

seen for what they are—
    mere attempted viability

snowdrifts of desires
    shedding thorns

near the windows
    where the breeze

blows in the evening
    dew

and heralds
    the coming storm

The Daggered Ice

      The edged blade—
it is not the dreaded decline
          that keeps us lying awake.
It is not the moaning menace
which forces us
     up the mountain top,
and holds us in suspense—

the soft dance of bird down—feathers
     as warm in the nest as when
we snuggled next to mother's breast,
is a haven where we huddled.

          now we hide in thermal divide—
mid-stride, and walking wide,
     lest we be drugged and dragged
dangerously onward or used as a weapon
    without our permission—which is not
a requirement to what happens in the world,
     nor a condition of concurrence,

with or without the daggered ice.
     it will merely suffice to provide the concise
contention—or intervention
for viability

January Wolf Moon

I found myself a voiceless bird,
hiding in the darkness, awake.
And the sound that filled the room
was the echo of my waking.
It was not fear that filled my throat;
this was not pain's blossom unfurling—
how they clamor in the mind,
heavy as feet ascending
a dark stairway.   But there is
at the top, a door
that opens onto a snowy field
lit by January's wolf moon.

There is joy in this night—see
how light plays blindingly
off suspended snowflakes;

See the silent birds lifting;
feel the deep cracking of ice
as it fills the void.

And ahead, thousands of songless
birds lifting their wings from the frozen
ground—taking flight.

A door behind me closes
quickly and forever,
beaten by wind, heat, time.
Suspended like the snowflakes.
I lift. I circle and fly. . .

A Single Sparrow

is it not part of God's design—
this cosmic intention?
Time is uncertain to men on earth,
hidden in the moment between past & future.

Yet the smallest space of redemption
can pass in a flash.
A sparrow shall not fall
without our father knowing.

The meanest flower that blows offers
thoughts that lie too deep for tears.
When paths cross at a particular point
in time and space the butterfly's

wings emerge, fill out and grow
as life's fluid is pumped into them.
And coming into the mystery
of it all—it is the thing itself.

Without death would we make
any significant choices?
Would we confront any limitations?
When our body is buried,

our ashes mix a new pattern
with the sand and wind and water;
our hearts flung into the void
to become newly minted.

What is the truer truth?
You will find no remedy for
the strength of love, nor
the length of death, yet—

what would we do with
immortality, anyway?

Dissolution
Achilles revisited

perhaps we unravel ourselves
as we live
and reassemble through
our demise.

birds sing an elegy without
learning the song—trusting the tune
will appear when needed;
dispensing life note by note.

the black water of the Styx covered us,
submerged us to our heels,
yet we are alive like Achilles,
left standing on the haunted beach.

we are unsolved mysteries,
extracting living essence daily,
feeling invulnerable, yet slain
with no man's weapon—our token of Hades.

from infancy to dust only divine
aid penetrates our skin—
our lives made viable
only with the dipping.

Death Is Not Personal

I plodded out to the end of my life,
slogged through the days and nights

of non-existence while
grief heaved alongside me.

Grief sat beside me, a pulsating thing
with large glove-covered hands.

I walked into this country,
this region of grief

on sluggardly time,
reimagined my old life

then withdrew into sorrow's obtuse light,
into the very heart of darkness

where it is only winter
and witnessed my own undoing.

Eventually, I arrived at the far side of grief
into the sunless residue

with this message:
Death is not personal.

When I die . . .

Lift Me Up

Say my name,
fill your cup
of time
with memories.

Sing my song,
yet be free
of sadness & despair—
don't go there
for too long.

See me in your
children's children—
in their tears
and laughter. Then, after
they are asleep

hold a memory
of me
you plan to keep.

Resources

National Alliance for Caregiving: Advancing family caregiving through research, innovation and advocacy at: www.caregiving.org

Eldercare Locator is a public service that provides an instant connection to resources that enable older persons to live independently in their communities at: www.eldercare.acl.gov

National Family Caregiver Support Program provides grants to states and territories to fund various supports that help family and informal caregivers care for older adults in their homes for as long as possible, through the Administration for Community Living at: https://acl.gov/programs/support-caregivers/national-family-caregiver-support-program

National Institute on Aging provides information on Alzheimer's and other illnesses associated with aging at: www.nia.nih.gov/health/alzheimers

Acknowledgments

"Fresh News" published in *Dreamers Creative Writing: Year 1 Anthology*, edited by Kat McNichol. First Paperback Edition, 2019.

"Gourmand of Orange" published in the *Pasque Petals*, spring 2020, South Dakota State Poetry Society and nominated for Pushcart Award by South Dakota State Poetry Society, fall 2020.

"Hard as Stone" published in *Minnesota Voices* booklet, summer 2020, Wadena MN, and in *Down in the Dirt Magazine*, via Scars Publications on October 2018. at: http://scars.tv/cgi-bin/framesmain.pl?writers and in *Down in the Dirt: Parallel Universe,* March/April 2019, Vol 163, Scars Publications. Published in *Pasque Petals*, April 2018. Printed in *ERR Artist Collective*, ERR-otta Zine, March 14, 2018.

"How Vast the Universe" published under the title "A Slim Polished Newness," by *OWS (Our Write Side)* Ink, LLC, Julia Allen, Head Editor, on the website for *Wednesday Words Series*, Feb 21, 2019, at: https://owsink.ourwriteside.com/2019/02/20/wednesday-words-a-slim-polished-newness-by-annette-gagliardi/

"Incubation" published in *Global Poemic: Kindred Voices on the era of COVID-19*, Live on Dec 6. 2020. at: https://globalpoemic.wordpress.com/2020/12/06/incubation/

"Lacuna" published in *Poetic Bond VIII*, November 2018.

"Mumbled Memories" published in T*he Silence Within*, 2001, in T*he sound of Poetry*, 2001, and in *The Best Poems & Poets of 2002*, 2002.

"Red Geraniums" published in *Open Your Eyes: A Poetry Anthology*, edited by Kevin Watt, Social Design Publishing, 2016.

"Rose Quartz Heaven" featured at *ERR Artist's Collective* and printed in their Zine, March 14, 2018, and printed in CosmographiaBooks.com anthology, 2018.

"She Was the Black Starling" published in *Wisconsin Review*, University of Wisconsin, Oshkosh, Spring 2021.

"This World Is a Grave" won Poem for the Month in May 2018, *Cosmographia* online poetry contest. Won $50.00 prize and published on the NinaAlvarez.net website. Published in *the spirit it travels, an anthology of transcendent poetry* edited by Nina Alvarez, *Cosmographia* 2018 anthology.

"Uses for Ashes" featured at *ERR Artist's Collective* and printed in their Zine, March 14, 2018.

Early Praise for
A Short Supply of Viability

In Annette Gagliardi's first collection of poetry, she squarely confronts universal aspects of the human condition. Joy, pain, regret, failing health, the passing of loved ones, and more, are addressed in accessible, down-to-earth detail that doesn't retreat from heartfelt emotion. Her earnest voice is at times incisive, sometimes somber, and at other times tender, as she takes the reader on a lifelong journey woven with a thread of spiritual hope for "viability".

—Alan Perry, author of *Clerk of the Dead*

Annette Gagliardi's *A Short Supply of Viability* takes an unflinching look at life and the hard facts of what it means to care for one who is slowly losing touch with life. These poems deftly reach for their subjects in the language of image and metaphor *giving way to a flowering darkness/ along with hours lost down the drain of the day.* Gagliardi asks us to not only to attend to what slips away from us in the daily, but to also behold these losses as fragments of song.

—Juliet Patterson, author of *Threnody* and *The Truant Lover*

Annette Gagliardi's dazzling poetry collection, *A Short Supply of Viability,* confronts mortality—our decline, our need for care, our love for life. Her preface defines *viability* as the ability to work, to survive, to live, to flourish, variations that thematically resound in her elegiac work, touching on the spiritual, the natural, the grief and consolation that accompany our journey on this earth. She mourns lost youth, lost parents even as she buoys our spirits, reminding us, as William Cullen Bryant does, to live: *If food is what you want, eat now* ("The Sea Shifts"). Her poems thrum with rich images of the natural world: *Small glimpses of who you/ used to be emerge—recede/*

[. . .]

like dolphins in the sea ("Grief in the Sail") or *the diminishing light/ pinpricks that bright vanishing/ into the landscape of stunned darkness* ("Mirage"). Ultimately, she embraces death as a lover, part of the natural order, reminding us in her beautiful poems that *vita brevis est*.

—Donna Isaac, author of *Persistence of Vision*; *Footfalls*; *Holy Comforter*; and *Tommy*

In her debut collection, Annette Gagliardi does not shy away from the difficult subject. Quite the contrary. The poems in *A Short Supply of Viability* take on death, dying, memory loss, and caregiving in language that is straightforward and humble in the face of the journey it strives to express. Witnessing decline and loss of loved ones, tending to their daily needs and comforts, occupy the spaces these poems sketch. They ask, *How do we carry on . . . ?* Then, in answer to their own question, they describe "Uses for Ashes," the transformation of firewood begetting soap, mulch bursting into hydrangeas' *truer, bluer blooms*. The speaker in these poems struggles in the short supply of the title. Nevertheless, *there is/at the top, a door/ that opens onto a snowy field*.

—Morgan Grayce Willow, author of *Dodge & Scramble*

About the Author

Annette Gagliardi is a Minnesota writer, author most recently of *Proper Poems for Ladies...and a few naughty ones, too!* She is a contributor and co-editor of *Upon Waking. 58 Voices Speaking Out from the Shadow of Abuse, 2019.* Annette has poetry published in *Motherwell, Wisconsin Review, American Diversity Report, Origami Poems Project, Amethyst Review, Door IS A Jar, Trouble Among the Stars, Poetry Quarterly, Sylvia Magazine,* and many other online and in-print magazines.

Find more of her work at https://annette-gagliardi.com/

About The Poetry Box®

The Poetry Box,® a boutique publishing company in Portland, Oregon, provides a platform for both established and emerging poets to share their words with the world through beautiful printed books and chapbooks.

Feel free to visit the online bookstore (thePoetryBox.com), where you'll find more titles including:

The Catalog of Small Contentments by Carolyn Martin

A Shape of Sky by Cathy Cain

A Long, Wide Stretch of Calm by Melanie Green

My Mother Never Died Before by Marcia B. Loughran

Let's Hear It for the Horses by Tricia Knoll

Late Fall Bucolics by Anne Coray

Sophia & Mister Walter Whitman by Penelope Scambly Schott

A Nest in the Heart by Vivienne Popperl

What We Bring Home by Susan Coultrap McQuin

Notes from a Caregiver by Meg Lindsay

Beneath the Gravel Weight of Stars by Mimi German

Tell Her Yes by Ann Farley

and more . . .

www.ingramcontent.com/pod-product-compliance
Lightning Source LLC
LaVergne TN
LVHW040107080526
838202LV00045B/3814